THE **JAMES BACKHOUSE** LECTURES

The lectures were instituted by Australia Yearly Meeting of the Religious Society of Friends (Quakers) on its establishment in 1964.

They are named after James Backhouse who, with his companion, George Washington Walker, visited Australia from 1832 to 1838. They travelled widely, but spent most of their time in Tasmania. It was through their visit that Quaker Meetings were first established in Australia.

Coming to Australia under a concern for the conditions of convicts, the two men had access to people with authority in the young colonies, and with influence in Britain, both in Parliament and in the social reform movement. In meticulous reports and personal letters, they made practical suggestions and urged legislative action on penal reform, on the rum trade, and on land rights and the treatment of Aborigines.

James Backhouse was a general naturalist and a botanist. He made careful observations and published full accounts of what he saw, in addition to encouraging Friends in the colonies and following the deep concern that had brought him to Australia.

Australian Friends hope that this series of Lectures will bring fresh insights into the Truth, and speak to the needs and aspirations of Australian Quakerism. This particular lecture was delivered at The Innovations Centre adjoining Wollongong East Campus, New South Wales in January 2011.

Maxine Cooper
Presiding Clerk
Australia Yearly Meeting

2011
THE **JAMES BACKHOUSE** LECTURE

A demanding and uncertain adventure

Exploration of a concern for Earth restoration and how we must live to pass on to our children – and their children, and all living things – an Earth restored

ROSEMARY (ROWE) MORROW

© The Religious Society of Friends (Quakers) in Australia, 2009.
eBook edition © 2011.

National Library of Australia Cataloguing-in-Publication entry:

Author: Morrow, Rosemary.

Title: A demanding and uncertain adventure [electronic resource] / Rosemary (Rowe) Morrow.

ISBN: 9780980325874 (pbk.)
          9780980325898 (ebook)

Series: James Backhouse lecture ; 2011

Notes: Includes bibliographical references.

Subjects: Religion and science.
          Science--Religious aspects.
          Spiritual life--Quakers.
          Permaculture.

Dewey Number: 261.55

Produced by Australia Yearly Meeting of the Religious Society of Friends (Quakers) in Australia Incorporated

Copies may be ordered from:
Friends Book Sales, PO Box 181
Glen Osmond SA 5064 Australia.
Email sales@ quakers.org.au
or from IP Sales: sales@ipoz.biz

About the author

Rosemary (Rowe) Morrow was born in Perth and grew up close to the Swan River and fell asleep at night to the sounds of lions roaring at the Perth Zoo. She ran away many times before she was five years old, mainly to see animals, such as a friend's goat or cow. And she has travelled with her work ever since. By eleven years old she was convinced that her life would be lived out in the very remote Outback. Well it wasn't, but from 16 to 21 years old she lived in the Kimberleys on the edge of the Tanami Desert where space, sand, sky and silence became lifelong values/necessities. Her friendships with Aboriginal Australians started then and have continued all her life.

Returning to Sydney she studied agriculture mistaking it for land care. Observant of Earth processes, Rowe grew aware and then alarmed by the rapid disintegration of Earth's ecosystems. She grieves for a damaged Earth; for every tree carelessly removed and every visible or invisible organism lost to extinction.

She trained in humanitarian work in France where she also lived in Trosly-Breuil l'Arche community, and in England at Jordan's where she knew she would become a Quaker. Most of the 1970s were spent in Lesotho. Back in Australia in the 1980s permaculture provided the powerful basis for

Earth restoration. A concern was born. She considers permaculture 'sacred' knowledge to be carried and shared with others. Since then she has travelled to meet many people anxious and concerned to restore their environments.

As a teacher of permaculture Rowe has been inspired for many years by Parker Palmer, the Alternatives to Violence Project (AVP) and non-violent resistance. She works in difficult places choosing people who have been disempowered and who would not otherwise have access to permaculture.

As an isolated Friend Rowe sits quietly on Sundays and joins spiritually with another Quaker meeting somewhere in the world on the same longitude. She joined Friends at the Devonshire Street Meeting and then the Blue Mountains where she made her home for many years. Being a lover of science she finds depths and challenges in Quakerism in the modern world of the 21st century, and particularly values the Quaker embrace of, and struggle with, continuing revelation.

Contents

About the author

Acknowledgements

Introduction: A letter to James Backhouse

    1. Australian adventurous pioneers in Earth repair   5

    2. Evolving Australian spiritual Earth relationships   10

    3. Responses to a damaged land   13

    4. Theological response to human failure to act   16

    5. Earth restoration as a concern   18

    6. Living well with less: how other cultures do it   27

    7. Permaculture: to restore the Earth   32

    8. Gardening the world back to health   35

    9. Spiritual darkness   43

    10. Slowing the descent: living adventurously   48

    11. The great unfolding Universe story   53

    12. The Great Work of restoration and reflection   56

References

Acknowledgements

This year of writing the Backhouse Lecture was a difficult one for me – more like an obstacle course than a smooth walk. It took some time to get the themes clear and when I did, personal family challenges intervened. It was a stop-go process and when I stopped or needed to start, there was always someone standing by with a prop and reassurance.

Past Backhouse lecturers reached out. Thank you David Johnston, Helen Gould and Helen Bayes for phone calls and assurances. And Sue Ennis introduced me to Parker Palmer and bought me all his books. How can I say thank you for that?

Of my writing group in Katoomba, Alison Gentle and Robyne Reichel read ill-prepared manuscripts and gave sound advice. Lis Bastion offered ideas and lead me to Penny. Elizabeth Kwan in Darwin took time from her demanding schedule to read and comment on one draft. James Strong sent wonderful emails and made me think. He generously provided the strong Quaker background enabling me to stretch my spirit and mind with confidence. The Backhouse Committee phoned me and Dale Hess was at the end of the phone or supportive email.

I live in happy obligation to all these people and thank them for their contributions. Their emotional and spiritual contributions were as great as the intellectual. And for those others by whom I have been delighted and provoked in our conversations, you are there on every page and I thank you as well and I am sorry not to give your names.

I dedicate this lecture to a beloved nephew, Michael, who loved all things living and would have been supportive and challenged by these times and this lecture.

Rosemary Morrow
November 2010

Introduction

A Letter to James Backhouse

Home

2nd Day, 4th month, 2010

Dear James Backhouse:

I am sorry that there is such a distance between us and we can't talk. But it is 179 years since you arrived in Australia and I have been asked to deliver the James Backhouse Lecture for the Australia Yearly Meeting in 2011. The world today is vastly changed yet you are a forebear and we share much in common and would have many things to talk about.

Are you gratified that an annual lecture commemorates your travelling under concern for convicts, Aboriginal people and the souls of women and men? Since its inauguration in 1964 there have been inspiring lectures.

I went to the Australian National Library (ANL) in Canberra, our national capital, to read your narratives of your travels in Australia, South Africa and Norway.

A librarian told me that I needed to read in a special room. I ordered your books and sat down. It was so quiet. I sat and breathed in and relaxed because my life had been very stressful.

The silence descended. I sat. They brought me a pencil, a pair of white cotton gloves and a soft cradle to put your books on so they wouldn't be damaged. I started to read. I turned the pages slowly and gradually my imagination moved into your life and times.

I started 'doing research' and finished after three days, sitting back in my chair and knowing that I had made friend for life. I felt comforted that some one else had known what it is to lead a life of travelling under concern. But what I had gone to your writings for – enlightenment about what a nurseryman and horticulturist of your times might say about Creation – was barely there.

But I found other riches.

James, you wrote much in your narratives that I, too, experienced over 20 or so years of travelling under concern. Some are trifling, such as the necessity of always having a handkerchief, and choosing to walk rather than accept other transport; and some are devastating, such as human brutality and despair.

And, perhaps it is a small thing, but you always called your concern 'your work' and I too, naturally used those words. Travelling under concern has been 'my work'.

I felt close to you because of the points of congruence in our lives. I thought: here is someone who knows what it is like to travel under concern for long periods of time, to places where people are kind but don't know you, and often are sceptical of your concern. Despite the time gap, the commonalities are greater than the differences especially where it touches on Quakerism.

Our first shared experience is that concerns are multi-faceted and interlinked. Your primary concerns flowed over to other inter-related issues such as food supplies, hunger and cruelty to animals. Our common ground covers:
- professions in agriculture and horticulture
- reading nature in three dimensions
- concern for justice and compassion for prisoners and Aborigines
- attention to food and hunger wherever it occurs
- caring how underprivileged people are treated
- abiding interest in education, especially orphans, adult education and science
- loneliness while travelling
- family tragedy

- religious beliefs tested and modified by suffering and evil
- sometimes despair and outrage at barbarous acts by humans.

Finally, we hold to Quaker practice and testimonies.

I have followed a singular path of concern for food, water and Earth repair, since realising in the mid-1980s that we are living lives of great risk because we are at the peak of Earth non-renewable resources such as fresh water, food, forests, and soil. My concern was possible because of a 20th century concept called permaculture, and the teaching and work of adult educators and the Alternatives to Violence Project.

I explore how implementing permaculture resolves many questions of development and problems of global warming. In projects first offered in Vietnam and Cambodia I did not know, and nor did Quaker Service Australia (QSA), that permaculture would be more than re-establishing food supplies for starving people. Permaculture, as more than gardening, proved to be a physical and social healer restoring peace, food, culture and self-respect to damaged people and landscapes. It provided a remembering of how to live again.

This lecture is about the Earth we share, how we live in it and where the Spirit is. We inherit many views about God and Nature, some strongly conservative, some revelatory and some contribute to the crisis we are in. Now in 2011, under pressure from science and psychology Earth theology has substantially changed.

By the end of the 20th century, many people's understanding, supported by science and theology, that Earth is on the brink of collapse came together with a new spiritual universe story, and gave to humans a great work – to restore Earth's ecosystems and biodiversity.

The Earth is in crisis but, in Australia, now a country of great wealth and luxury, we don't feel it pressingly yet. I think it would be hard for you to see much of the destruction. It is painful for me.

I found Earth-sustainable principles in five traditional cultures. There are no technical impediments to Earth restoration except human willingness that now would require considerable sacrifices such as:

- living frugally
- building peaceful communities
- putting Earth's web of relationships at the heart of restoration.

So you see, at the centre is a spiritual view of life as sacred.

As a sub-theme I looked at the impact of Quakers and the impact on Quakers. I think that Quakers, if they wanted to, could model sustainable living on Earth.

It is late, nearly midnight, and the wind is spitting big drops of rain on my tin roof and then pauses to take breath and starts again. Other than that the world is very quiet.

James Backhouse, thank you for walking with me on this rocky path over the last months. I was baffled until I read your journal and discovered a soul mate. We have many differences but our concerns are for things that are eternal. It has been good to write to you.

There are challenging times with difficult questions and huge changes ahead.

In peace, friendship and gratitude,
Your Friend,
Rosemary (Rowe) Morrow

P.S. By the way, you are still spoken of today. A neighbour, sent me this:

This morning on local radio I heard a local historian talking about a James Backhouse, a Quaker who went over the Blue Mountains in the 1830s to Bathurst. A couple of weeks later when returning through Richmond he mentioned having been to Bathurst to an Aboriginal man, who told him he already knew that he, Backhouse, had been there spreading the word. When Backhouse asked him what the message had been he was told 'God Almighty sat down at Bathurst'.[1]

1 Shirley Brown in an email of 5th day, sixth month, 2009

1. Australian adventures in Earth repair

We depend on the trees and animals
We depend on the earth
We live in all things
All things live in us.
Stephanie Kaza, Green Gulch Farm

I was born just before the age of massive increase in the speed of extraction and use of resources. In 1953 I was a ten year-old returning from burying myself in the warm sands of the quiet beaches of the Swan River; walking home in bare feet on hot asphalt, swinging my towel, smelling the boronia and lingering.

Later, in Sydney I was running around the harbour, listening to tugboats hooting in the fog at Cremorne and Neutral Bay. I swam at Northbridge and went home to Castlecrag through the bush, stopping to lie like a lizard on warm sandstone rocks. There was always a flowering wattle to smell.

Earth, through the rocks, textures, plants, and scents had claimed me as it had others.

In the early years of the 20th century in Australia there emerged a few 'bioneers' passionate about a restorative relationship with unlikely landscapes. And during the 1950s, 1960s and 1970s they were still largely unknown and yet deeply engaged in what they recognised as damaged landscapes. They probably did not know of each other's work yet I would inherit their pioneering endeavours.

In Broken Hill, Bertie Morris saw the inter-relationships among plants, wind and water and how together they protected and tied firmly the Earth's skin, the soil.

A silver mining industry had begun in the desert at Broken Hill. Among its new residents in 1890, 14 year-old Albert 'Bertie' Morris was deeply marked by watching the drifting sands and dust storms move into the city. He watched his father build a big stone wall to keep out the sand. Within a short time the sand came to the top of the wall.

Later he saw how further 'development' of the Silver City stripped the surrounding hills for mine props, fuel for cooking, heating, smelting, and buildings, leaving its hills denuded. The sand rolled in and dust storms increased. Bertie became convinced that only restoration of the original vegetation could hold down the profligate sands and prevent them from enveloping the city. Initially, his ideas were discounted.

In 1909 he married Quaker Margaret Sayce, and later became a Quaker himself. He developed the idea of a green belt around the city that, he asserted, would not only help but wholly remove the problem. Assisted by Edwin Ashby, a leading South Australian Quaker botanist[1], he experimented for many years with plants for dry areas.

Today, a collar of green encircles Broken Hill. His success and vision travelled. Israelis and Americans came to see the results and his methods were copied in other countries. The methods he advocated are among those recommended as best practice in land restoration.

The outback called me and in 1959 I left Sydney to follow my dream to live on an outback cattle station and it was at Gordon Downs Station, on the edge of the Tanami Desert, that I became dimly aware of a remarkable woman living in Alice Springs.

A Tasmanian Quaker, Olive Muriel Pink, born in 1884, was an anthropologist and botanic artist who fell in love with the native plants around Alice Springs.[2] An agitating and passionate advocate for improved Aboriginal rights in the 1930s and 1940s she campaigned forcefully for them and was critical of missionaries, government officials and pastoralists.

After 36 years living in the Tanami desert she began work on a plant reserve in Alice Springs and in 1956 she and her Warlpiri assistant gardeners established public gardens for the appreciation of central desert indigenous plants. Having no money she grew her own fruit and flowers, exhibited her artwork and refused the Old Age Pension.

In the Australian Arid Region Flora Reserve she gave each plant a name and if a person was out of favour the plant was not watered. She helped begin Yuendemu Aboriginal Art Outstation community. She received Quaker support in 1942[3] and lived in her garden in a galvanised shed until she died in 1975 aged 91.

She needed tenacity to act against prevailing opinions on Aboriginal rights and the value of desert plants. She held close ties to Quakers all her life and is buried in the Quaker section of the Alice Springs cemetery.

While she was planting her Reserve, I was in the Kimberleys where station managers scornful of their bush heritage were pouring bore water onto exotic plants to make the homesteads 'beautiful' and change the local habitat to make it fit to grow plants from other cultures and climates.

In 1988 I visited the Olive Pink Australian Arid Region Reserve and was in awe of her struggle and vision in protecting the thorny, dull grey and glaucous greens expressing the shy exquisite nature of arid land plants[4] that I loved greatly.

Red Mitchell, an American Quaker, who migrated to Australia and joined the Blue Mountains Local Meeting, was a silviculture graduate. During the Second World War he was interned as a conscientious objector and worked in the National Park in Hawaii. Long before Rachel Carson's book, *Silent Spring*, he wrote about a meeting he attended where it was intended to introduce new insecticides into the environment.[5] On 14th October 1944, he wrote in a letter that should have aroused alarm:

I stood up for the insects. I defended them. I told of the wondrous beauty of even the least of God's creatures. Now man proposed to destroy them – some species to extinction, perhaps all. None of the experts spoke to me after that, perhaps I should have sat silent, looking wise …

And then in the 1960s and 1970s along the Sydney foreshore within sound and sight of the Harbour Bridge, two sisters walked through the bushland each day. **Joan and Eileen Bradley**[6], systematic observers of the natural environment, studied the habits of three families of the Superb Fairy Wren. When numbers fell dramatically in 1966, Joan alerted the press that minute doses of organochlorines over long periods caused sterility in small birds. They also developed the principles and practices that would become 'bush regeneration'. By 1975 this had gained the support of the National Trust and conservation associations and is now an Australian applied science vocation.[7] Variations of the Bradley method have been adopted around the world.

Meanwhile in the 1970s I was intellectually blundering around, gaining more academic knowledge in Europe and then being largely ineffective in Lesotho. But another concept was being developed which would change my life and give me a vocation.

In the 1970s, two ecologists at the University of Tasmania, **Bill Mollison** and **David Holmgren**, were working on an Earth-friendly innovation – permaculture – whose importance in Earth restoration I discuss later. They had seen the ravages of clearfell forestry, and soil, water and species loss. They had seen towns and cities fouled by coal polluting industries. They drew on many threads from society and the environment to develop a fabric of ethics, principles and strategies for Earth restoration and longterm sustainability.

The restorative methods of Bertie Morris, Olive Pink and the Bradley sisters were gentle and patient. They paced restoration to the seasons and allowed the land to dictate its rate of recovery. They worked with Earth and her time. This was revolutionary but they probably did not realise how critical intact, permanent natural systems and biodiversity are for climate stability. Mollison and Holmgren did know, and consciously created repair principles.

These Australian 'bioneers' spiritual insights saw and respected all ecological interactions. They became convinced that Earth, if permitted, can heal herself. Pleasing to Quaker beliefs is that they acted on their insights. They would provide my vocation and the vehicle for Quaker concern.

But in Australia in the late 19th and early 20th century, bush poets wrote about rural conditions and the pioneer spirit of rural men, women, and animals. It was a case of battling the bush, subduing and transforming it into images of European landscape. Their attitudes reflected a masculine and adversarial God who would send a drought or flood to correct the sinners who then went to church to repent. They had a conflicted relationship with Australia, regarding it as harsh. They blamed the land for droughts and floods, not inappropriate farming methods and ill-adapted crops from Europe.

Examples of working with the Earth were rare and by the second half of the 20th century most Australians were no longer earning their living in intimacy with the land which fed them and were distant from such practices.

Chapter 1 notes

1 Edwin Ashby 1861-1941 was a South Australian botanist and Quaker. He was also a collector of birds, butterflies, shells, chitons (recent and ancient fossils). The best of these were donated to the SA Museum. He became fascinated by Australian native flora and opened a native plant nursery in the 1930s to preserve wildlife. His property 'Wittunga' was given to the Botanical Gardens in Adelaide. His daughter Alison was a distinguished collector and painter of Australian Flora.Bib.ID 1567-745 State Library.

2 A town in the centre of Australia, often called the Red Heart for its arid climate and extremes of weather. It was for many years seen as inhospitable. Today it lives on fossil water and imports everything.

3 http://www.opbg.com.au/2010/about-miss-pink/

4 1st June 2010, ABC Radio National dedicated one hour to Olive Pink and her achievements.

5 Private email from Elizabeth Mitchell, 4th June 2010, Red Mitchell's unpublished diary. Red Mitchell became an Australian and member of Blue Mountains Local Meeting

6 adbonline.anu.edu.au/biogs/A130275b.htm

7 I belong to two bushcare groups in the Blue Mountains where we have 64 groups of happy regenerators.

2. Evolving spiritual Earth relationships

The voyage of discovery is not in seeking new landscapes but in having new eyes.
Marcel Proust

But some Australians turned blame into appreciation and some, to love. In 1953, Rudolf Lemberg, scientist, Australian migrant and Quaker, wrote a current view of God's image in nature:

> *I have beheld the beauties of creation in mountains, rock and glacier, gleaming sunlight and floating clouds, the glittering seashore of my new home, the virgin beauty of alpine and bushland flowers, beauty in colour and song of birds and the teeming life of the seashore rock pool, yes, even in toad and snake.*

He experienced that God as knowable through nature, and that God is good. This is now common ideology for Earth theologians for whom, as worshipping human observers, to *do no harm* became an imperative.

A modern critique of this belief by George Sessions[1] is that *We keep nature at arm's length when we just look at it as scenery*. But it was this gratitude and worship of God, beautiful and visible that would thrust many Australians, Quakers among them, into non-violent activism to protect forests and wilderness.

John Ormerod Greenwood, Backhouse Lecturer in 1982[2], made a theological leap when he presented a radical view of place as sacred and utterly rejected the desecration of sacred natural places. The natural wilderness he experienced connected humans with the 'unseen'.

Though I believe as a Quaker that all places, times and seasons are equally sacred I, at the same time believe and no inconsistency in this – that there are places, times and seasons that are especially sacred ... that Ayers Rock – Uluru –and other places of worship of the Australian Aborigines are especially sacred and there is no way in which desecration of them can be justified ... They are sacred because at these places and these times, men have regularly and with sacrifice and devotion penetrated the veil that separates us from the unseen.

The inanimate joined the living as sacred. Earth was being seen differently. And for some people, so was Australia.

By the late 20th century as understanding grew of the rapidly increasing human destructive impact on Earth, Quakers like Francis Hole (1995) were writing passionately and prolifically in defence, praise and wonder of a *living Earth*. Francis[3] writes of being exhorted by the Divine Presence to love and appreciate not only plants and other creatures but earth, snow and rocks.

It is as if the Divine Presence said to us, 'Ever seek balance ... You are to love and appreciate yourself, other persons, plants and creatures around you, stars, earth, snow and rocks.

Do not 'fall in love' with any of these to be possessed by them and swallowed up; neither turn away from them, nor renounce them. In the balance that you attain, keep me ever in view.

Some Quakers felt uneasy about such specificity and the expression of divine love for inanimate objects.

However by the end of the 20th century natural adversity was still seen as inherently the land's or the climate's fault, but not ours. Australians were still saying they lived in a *harsh land* and deploring what Nature/God was doing.

And Australia was very damaged.

Woomera was a rocket site. Monte Bello, Emu Field and Maralinga were the sites of the British atomic tests. Woomera closed for 1,000 or is it 10,000 years; the uranium mines, vast strip coal mining, the empty and dying rivers polluted and cleared of life; some of the greatest species loss in the world; and of serious consequence for future generations, massive depletion of water tables; the highest non-renewable energy use per head in the world; and deserts where before there had been vast woodlands.

Valuable and irretrievable soils carelessly escape into the rivers and seas. Oceans are being fished to extinction. Some ecosystems can never be returned to their pristine fullness.

Of most concern is the atmosphere into which we have poured unconscionable amounts of carbon dioxide destabilising ten thousand years of climate stability. This is the time of global warming.

Chapter 2 notes

1 Sessions, George and Duvall. W. *Living as if Nature Mattered*, /www.transnational-perspectives.org/transnational/articles/article36.pdf

2 John Ormerod Greenwood, Backhouse Lecture, 1982, *Celebration, a Missing Element in Quaker Worship.*

3 Francis Hole, *A Little Journal of Devotions out of Quaker Worship*, Quaker Press, 2001.

3. Responses to a damaged land

Sometimes our Light goes out but is blown into flame by another human being. Each of us owes deepest thanks to those who rekindled this Light.
Albert Schweitzer

Paradoxically, as her resources were being depleted and global warming threatened, Australia in the 20th century was becoming loved passionately. Strong and passionate advocates emerged around political, social and environmental issues. Attitudes were changing. Australia, far from being harsh, punitive and unforgiving, was fragile, diverse, had a shy delicate beauty and was essentially resilient. Australia, appreciated as a storehouse of unique natural riches and not simply a commodity or a museum, made some people question utilitarianism.

Visionaries were seeking and finding Spirit and coherence in the land – bushwalkers, campers, hermits, gardeners, diarists, musicians, artists, photographers, poets, writers, film-makers, scientists, theologians, academics and, a new political party – the Greens. Early in the 20th century bushwalkers agitated for and gained the first National Parks.

The Australian war against Vietnam added to people power in the 1970s. Citizens agitated and demonstrated. Television took issues into homes. Growing demands from aware and mindful hearts were expressed in early *eco-consciences* leading to Green Bans, and protection of forests, the Antarctic, the Great Barrier Reef and deserts.

Thus the Franklin still runs free and perhaps, one day, Lake Pedder will be returned to the Tasmanian landscape. The Great Barrier Reef is now a marine National Park.

I rather think it would surprise James Backhouse that fierce environmental battles took place in Tasmania in the 20th and 21st centuries where national historical precedents were set by non-violent action to preserve the very wilderness that he had found so threatening. Quakers of the 20th century participated in the non-violent defence of wilderness forests.

There was a new appreciation that human and ecological rights and needs differ and Earth ecosystems must follow their own natural evolution.

Rejecting a worldview of endless economic growth, acquisition of material wealth and seeing a spiritual crisis, some people felt shame for past actions and ignorance and acknowledged responsibility for:
- disrupting sensitive ecosystems
- air pollution
- reducing biodiversity
- overloading pollutants
- depleting materials
- diminishing species and losing biodiversity
- depriving future generations of their birthright.

They were called 'greenies' and were ridiculed by many but were helped by a new measure, the ecological footprint which revealed:
- startling inequities
- imbalance in consumption
- how fast Earth is degrading
- where responsibility lies
- where change must come from.

The footprint, still a prototype, is accurate enough to tell us that each Australian takes about 6.7 hectares of arable land to meet all their needs. A child in Bangladesh uses 0.2 hectares. A fair and equitable measure is 1.8 hectares for every person on Earth.

Earth's highly educated, greatest consumers have brought her to the brink of collapse through a profligate use of resources. Restoration is the primary responsibility of the greatest consumers and polluters but it will take the co-operation of all to survive.

And, excluded from the material wealth, Aboriginal people never ceased their spiritual cry, pursued land rights and mourned their exile from the land to which they belong.

4. Theological responses to human failure to act

We are like trees, we must create new leaves,
in new directions, in order to grow.
Anonymous

It appears we humans cannot to be trusted with a role of power and dominion over Creation. We have failed. Having put the future of all life at risk it is not valid to talk about being stewards of Creation. Some Quakers in the 1980s and 1990s changed spiritual beliefs to accommodate the dreadful understanding that we live with huge risk and can no longer deny that we are part of the problem.

Friends in the USA were quicker than Australian Friends to develop an Earthcare Testimony. They also began Friends in Unity with Nature (FUN).

UK Quakers felt that the underlying causes were spiritual, and brought together Quaker Green Concern basing it on John Woolman's declaration that *We live answerable to the design of ... creation.*

They wrote, Quakers believe that:

The whole of life is sacramental
That spirit and action are indivisible
That there is always the real possibility of personal and social transformation
That human power over nature should not be used irresponsibly.

For the first flowering of Earth-conscious writing Australian Quakers have to thank Canberra Meeting in 1996 for producing *Quakers and Nature* and the pamphlet which preceded it.

From the study of ecology and other sciences, ideas of ecosystem interdependence and interrelationship entered theology through Earth theologians such as Thomas Berry in the USA, leading to sacred relationship with Earth, not ownership or domination. Without relationship with living and non-living species there can be no sustainable future. For this future we need to make the fundamental change from ownership to relationship through

- relationships that exhibit intimacy, reciprocity and love for sacred Earth
- full understanding of the requirements of the human role.

These two issues occupy the last part of this lecture.

5. Earth restoration as a concern

It is time to sit down and be still,
for you are very drunk,
and we are at the edge of the roof.
Rumi

It is confronting to be the species with capacity for reflection that cannot control its wants and greed. When, in the late 1980s I became aware what our behaviour meant I went to my Quaker meeting and asked for spiritual guidance. I was terrified by the knowledge and the probability of another great extinction, like the previous five but this time caused by conscious human activity.

My meeting's suggestion to work with the testimony to simplicity and Quaker queries and advices on Earthcare did not assuage my fears. I grew heavy, losing my belief in 'that of God in everyone'. I started searching for a spirituality reaching further back than 2000 years and one that would compassionately offer a creative role for repair and stability.

The short life of Christianity started to look like the blink of a gnat's eye.

From reading the Bible I decided that Christianity does not teach us our place in creation and we have stopped observing, interacting with, and loving Earth. We have stopped talking about the things that are eternal. I knew intuitively that,

> *Only when we perceive that we are part of the totality of the planet, not a superior part with special privileges, can we work effectively to bring about an earth restored to wholeness.*

We needed to see ourselves only as cells in the *burning oneness binding everything* that Kenneth Boulding[1] describes in Sonnet I.

> *And yet, some Thing that moves among the stars,*
> *And holds the cosmos in a web of law,*
> *Moves too in me: a hunger, a quick thaw*
> *Of soul that liquefies the ancient bars,*
> *As I, a member of creation sing*
> *The burning oneness binding everything.*
> **Sonnet 1, The Nayler Sonnets**

In this moving poem by the 20th century American Quaker I find my spirituality. It is in the world, and cosmological understanding. I have profound faith in the spirituality inherent at the birth of our universe and which has moved in tandem with it. I am held tightly by its threads in a relationship with all life and now my faith is: *it is not how the world is, but that it is, and this is mystical.* And this spirituality underpins my concern.

I am not sure that James Backhouse would recognise my concern as a concern. His was to look into and report on the condition of convicts and Aborigines, and he preached to save the souls of women and men. I have not saved one soul and yet I think most Friends today would recognise my work as a concern. I don't preach because I wouldn't know what to say. Also our present day Australian Quaker culture is not one of preaching. We have become silent about saving souls. And for both James Backhouse and me plants enliven the solitude and beguile the walk.

Teaching to restore Earth is my concern. *These words by Parker Palmer[2], teaching is something I could not – not do, for reasons I am unable to explain to anyone else and don't fully understand myself but that are nonetheless compelling...* are almost identical to Backhouse's[3] words... *The belief that we were in our right place was sustaining.*

This is where my heart and soul stood.

As a permaculturist my concern for Earth restoration is an umbrella for Quaker[4] testimonies on peace and right livelihood and exercises the testimonies to integrity and community. My small understanding tells me my ecological vocation is to share knowledge and skills for Earth restoration with those least able to access it.

Despite years of development people suffer loss and deprivation of basic needs and natural systems and have difficulty in accessing useful relevant knowledge, and equity of wealth, skills, access to resources and basic necessities. So I have two parts to my concern.

- to offer relevant knowledge and skills to enable Earth repair
- to transfer that information in ways that are respectful and mindful of people's lives and culture.

Growth and development of a concern

It began in 1973 when I abandoned a newly begun PhD in Montpellier to go to a small grey stone village in the north-east of France to live in the community of L'Arche. French friends introduced me to L'Arche and its founder, Jean Vanier, who had been inspired to advocate for adults with intellectual disability.

At this time intellectually disabled people were incarcerated in grim psychiatric asylums. Jean Vanier had men and women released into his care, offering them a life of *le petit homme dans la rue*; that is, an ordinary life of privacy, freedom, work, leisure and community. Jean called volunteers from all around the world to become 'assistants' for his new residents. And I became one.

We lived with them and learned that people who have been rejected and are often inarticulate, hold different values. Because they have never had to compete intellectually, nor strive for physical beauty, many retain insightful clarity into life.

My unconscious values were shaken. Although I stayed only one year, it was time enough to be sensitised to the value of people the world avoids. My spiritual education had begun but my vocation still was not clear although I knew I belonged to the Earth.

I studied rural sociology in France, and overseas humanitarian work at Reading University where I found Jordan's village and Quakers. In my first meeting for worship I knew I would become a member and I began to read about Quakerism, but five years would pass before I could attend meetings in Australia and apply for membership.

In those five years I lived in Maseru, Lesotho on the edge of the town and there, in a settlement/slum, I learned how little control is in the hands of very poor people.

To be poor in Lesotho

Children dropped out of school because there was no money for fees. People died because they couldn't afford a doctor, and they died in the hospital that was filthy and had no medicines.

People were late for work because of the mud, or the minibus didn't arrive, or the baby burnt itself badly on the kerosene stove, and dogs owned by rich people were taught to attack them.

There were two taps outside for about 20 people and no drainage for water from clothes, dishes and teeth washing. Families lived in one room. Six people lived in the one small room beside me. I was the only person with a room to myself.

The obstacles impinging on the lives of poor people are endless – from inequality of knowledge and resources, to blatant injustice.

Like most Australians I was raised with access to knowledge, resources and a buffer zone against homelessness, hunger, and thirst. I bought my food on Saturday mornings from the little market in Maseru. The women sat with their few tomatoes, a couple of potatoes, some knobbly carrots and, that's about all. I, meanwhile, talked to other expatriates about growing asparagus for the South African market.

I was blind. I couldn't see that these tiny harvests from a woman's garden were all she had to raise money for school fees or painkillers. She was selling the food her family needed to eat. I could not see her hunger. And in my housing block I could not see what to do about water even though we had so little.

My extensive education was useless and I was not equipped to see, much less solve, the problems of hunger and thirst. My university degree in agriculture was as useful as a bucket of sand to a desert. I learned a hard lesson in Lesotho and I returned to Australia. I applied for membership of New South Wales Regional Meeting. I didn't know it then, but I was walking the same road as James Backhouse.

I found that a concern evolves, stretches and changes us.

My concern unfolded over 13 years from L'Arche, France to permaculture in Australia. And I may not have realised it if I had not become a Quaker in 1979. The concern was multi-faceted and I had much to do to realise it.

I started my search.

I enrolled in horticulture to learn how to build gardens, use tools and grow plants. I grew more aware of the destruction of natural ecosystems and the loss of species, soil, fresh water and, even food. I decided to learn how to conserve these rapidly diminishing ecosystems. I saw the conflict between destruction to meet human uses and needs of natural systems. Could the two be reconciled?

Then I found permaculture and I saw it covered most issues of environmental and social sustainability and would work in Kathmandu, Katoomba or Kolkata. I decided to take this knowledge to people who lacked access to it. I would work in humanitarian work although it is complicated with many strands and motives.

So now I digress a little to explore development.

Development, a worldwide industry carried out by NGOs,[5] grew out of

18th century missionary work from the days when people of different cultures and history were seen as needy, uncivilised or primitive. Today it refers to a fuzzy concept called poverty.

The drive to develop derives from attitudes that other cultures should:
- live European lifestyles
- become globalised and speak English
- join the growth economy, mainly through credit
- buy our goods
- govern themselves as we do
- run their health and education systems as we do
- sell us their raw materials cheaply.

These ideas can be terrifyingly destructive. There has been 'development' for more than 100 years and some recipient countries are poorer today than before.[6]

Poverty has many facets, including environmental poverty, and I set out to untangle it. I learned by experience why people are hungry, thirsty and destroy the natural environment, and why they must constantly focus on meeting their basic needs.

In Vietnam, apart from the legacy of war,

The area of land needed to grow food can be impossibly small, even with increases in productivity such as an extra crop.
- A code of land inheritance and tenure results in unequal division land. Some people have to walk half a day between plots with heavy tools and cannot give each plot equal care.
- In some provinces HIV/AIDS, out-migration from villages, environmental degradation, polluted waters, and debt to moneylenders who charge up to 60 per cent per annum interest, crush families.
- In Central Vietnam cyclones have increased from the manageable two or three a year, to five or six with destruction of crops too frequent to be supportable.

In East Timor
- As tenants, either of the Catholic Church or the expatriate Portuguese, farmers must pay rent and have few land rights.
- Years of war and colonial invasion destroyed homes, markets, farms and families and trust in a peaceful future.
- Language policies restrain communication and education.

In Afghanistan
- 500,000 internally displaced refugees in camps are villagers relying on food hand-outs or scavenging.
- So many men have been killed that women and children are left without protection.
- Children in orphanages in Kabul are poor because of the terrible things they experienced.
- Invading armies, present and past, destroyed 3,000 year-old traditional food production systems based on snowmelt irrigation.

In Australia:
- Land and farmers become poorer through debt, land degradation, global warming and destruction of water resources.

My priority was to become proficient in harvesting, using and maintaining water purity in all circumstances, because poverty is directly linked to access to water. Food was the next urgent issue and I had to learn how to grow food under difficult conditions.

And there are two world fuel crises directly affecting wellbeing.
- In the affluent world, the depletion of liquid fuel reserves threatens lifestyles. Prices will rise because the resource is finite. Initially, the price rise will affect holidays or a trip to the shop for a loaf of bread, but in the long term it will affect every aspect of life.
- The second is a survival issue in countries where cities, lacking other fuel resources, like vast vacuum cleaners suck in charcoal and timber

from sparsely timbered rural areas for cooking and heating. The effort to obtain charcoal or timber for fuel devours women's lives particularly. The trees so needed by the air, soil and rivers, are hewn, burned and not replaced. When this diminishing resource finally fails, the distress already being felt will be unbearable.

In my mind are pictures of desolate inland Mozambique with its bleak, arid, war-torn hills, empty landscape and an economy based on making charcoal. The people sell grilled mice and small birds on sticks to passers-by. Otherwise they starve.

The other form of poverty is from lack of access to relevant information that enables good decisions, and ameliorates present and future risks. Millions of people cannot access
- information on the likely impact and consequences of global warming
- information to earn a living or grow one, harvest water and restore landscapes
- support to retain indigenous culture and history
- weather warnings to avoid or endure disasters
- materials to prevent diseases such as HIV/AIDS and malaria.

I know that humanitarian projects that do not restore the environment are not development. This excludes many projects normally seen as successful, e.g. income generation schemes; Chinese roads in Ethiopia and Cambodia; chemical-dependent farming in Africa; water projects which use bores for rice production.

I did not know how to collate the information I would need nor how to deliver skills and information in ways that were culturally sensitive and learner-centred. I struggled along the 'development' road. My spirit never questioned it. My mind often did, especially when I was homesick. I always live the tension between wanting to be home and wanting to be away. And I had to find out how peoples had lived sustainably when resources are naturally meagre.

Chapter 5 notes

1 Kenneth Boulding is an outstanding 20th century Quaker who contributed in ideas and action to worship and peace. He wrote Sonnets based on the first line of Nayler's poem. flipkart.com/there-spirit-kenneth-boulding-nayler-book-1432580914

2 Parker Palmer is a present day US Quaker with a concern for teaching, learning and education. He has been a favourite writer of mine for more than ten years.

3 Backhouse, James. A narrative *A Visit To The Australian Colonies*, Hamilton Adams and Co. Paternoster Row, York MDCCCXLIII

4 We are fortunate to have Mark Deasey's *Backhouse Lecture* as a background to development work and our testimonies and ethics informing development.

5 ibid.

6 When I left Lesotho 30 years ago, life expectancy was about 48 years; now it is 32 years. This is true for much of Africa which has received humanitarian projects for a long time.

6. Living well with less: how other cultures do it

Wherever you are is home
And Earth is paradise
Wherever you set your feet is holy land.
William Pelletier and Ted Poole [1]

My special interest is in dry land restoration and food production because Australia, the driest continent, is becoming hotter and drier. Most of us perceive this as a looming disaster, but other cultures have not found aridity disheartening. There are many possible responses. Despite sparse soils, few plants and animals and a lack of water, some cultures have always found their 'country' good. They understood life as cyclic and they lived in close appreciative relationships with their lands.

As an Australian listening to constant voices of grievance about our natural climate, soils and plants, I wanted to know whether it is possible to live rich lives in a 'poor' environment. I wanted to know if there were universal principles. I searched for cultures that live well with less, and found five remarkable cultures.

Traditional Aboriginal living enthralled by the land's intangible properties.

Thinking about Australia, in *Treading Lightly*[2], one question challenged me:

How could the burra ground [in north-western New South Wales] for sacred ceremonies have sustained about 15,000 people where today on this land a few lanky cattle now rummage the parched earth to find the handfuls of grass still left?

The authors say,

The land looked distinctly different in those times. The river carried more water and was distinctly deeper. No property owners pumped water away and the river's clear edge would have been teeming with fish and unhindered by weirs. The surrounding land benefited from floods twice a year which refilled the soil and meant there was edible vegetation for both people and animals. The deep waterholes kept water and sustained fish populations,

The world, as we know it, was of little importance to the Nhunggabarra. Instead they were enthralled by their land's intangible properties. What they saw with their own eyes – the landscape, rock, rock outcrops, plains, mountains, waterholes – had been left behind by their Ancestors. The land gave them food but the Nhunggabarra were equally interested in its power to evoke the spiritual side of nature. The land was full of symbolic images reminding them about creation, immortality, sacred law and, most significantly, their role within the cosmic process itself.

Tex Scuthorpe and Karl-Erik Sveiby[3] describe how the Nhunggabarra people saw their land after 40,000 years – time enough to evolve a balanced and spiritual life. For them there was no omnipotent, omniscient God. Instead they knew that the spiritual and material were inextricably connected. The life view was cyclic not linear or evolving.

Today, Aboriginal people[4] see a *landscape in corruption* and call it *the age of destruction of ecosystems* as non-Aboriginals battle to make the land approximate a northern hemisphere landscape.

The paradox is that in their efforts to achieve abundance and wealth, non-Aboriginals destroy that which existed naturally. They impose destructive processes from a cultural mindset and are blind to the abundance that once existed.

At the Devonshire Street Quaker Meeting House in Sydney some years ago there was a meeting with Aboriginal people. Disturbed, I went outside. A young Aboriginal man joined me and said:

> *You know what? When you whitefellas arrived you looked at this place and saw chaos and said that we didn't know how to farm it. You cut the trees and built fences. But then it rained and flooded and you built dams and then it didn't rain and so you said there was a drought. You brought disorder and chaos to this land. We, blackfellas, we didn't have fences; when it rained we spread out widely across the land and hunted and ate well. When it didn't rain, we came closer to the sea and rivers and stayed there, and we hunted and ate well. We lived in harmony with the land.*

The Konso elegantly adapted

Recently in Ethiopia with Amanda Cuyler[5] and the Konso people who live in walled villages with terraced fields at the head of the Rift Valley, we documented the unrecorded beliefs and strategies they used over six centuries to survive well in one of the most unpredictable climates in the world. They responded to unpredictable water, soil, slopes, forests, food and animal population by limiting consumption of their resources when they were scarce; and at these times sharing is mandatory, with priority to the young and the ill. They respected and honoured every part of this natural world they found good and beautiful.

The Papago had to coax their existence

This little known Native American tribe[6] lived forever in a land of little rain, the Sonoran Desert in Arizona. This small population of about 16,000 developed the wisdom to keep their population in step with the carrying capacity of the lowest and hottest of the North American deserts from which they had to coax their existence. But home for them is not a dry, scorched, monotonous land – it is a world of endless contrasts where the miracles of water are readily perceived. In this environment the Spirit of Goodness, I'itoi, watches over them. The Spanish missionaries spoke of the Papago as living 'on sterile lands' and as 'being naked and very poor'. The Papago saw themselves as living in one of the most blessed lands on Earth.

Faced with little, Papago practise generosity – the greatest virtue. They lived lightly on the land ... demonstrated an unwillingness to waste the desert's most precious asset, its water. Poor as the country was, its economics were those of abundance. They did not hoard property ... they were constantly giving as though from an inexhaustible supply ... meagre though it was, it was sufficient for their simple needs and more. Food was the principal gift. The standard meal was cornmeal gruel: luxuries much beyond that were donated with lavish hand and never missed. Anyone who gained the reputation for stinginess damned his prospects in village and family life, while the lavish giver not only achieved honour but had continual income pouring in.

The Bishnoi were the first eco-martyrs

Years ago[7] I became fascinated by these people of the Rajasthan Desert who live bountifully in a rainfall of often less than 2.0 cm per year. They match consumption to the land's productivity. They consider their country rich and blessed. They never cut trees and became the first eco-martyrs when they died trying to stop interlopers from felling them.

The San bushmen of the Kalahari[8] found depth, wonder and goodness in their desert. They worshipped perhaps the smallest God, Mantis. The stars and sand and small things were of unending fascination. They lived lives of voluntary thrift and limited their consumption.

The unifying principles in these surviving resilient cultures are prophetic and, paradoxically derived from the past, they indicate ways to live in the future. Looking for guidelines for how to live in Australia in a drier and unpredictable future I found environmental pressures create similar

principles, and people survive because they
- find their land good and bountiful
- adapt and respond swiftly to changing environmental conditions
- limit and control consumption
- practise generosity
- practise co-operation and community
- limit carrying capacity so Earth can heal and restore herself
- celebrate and honour life.

How would our lives change if we were respectful of this dry continent and found its natural fires, floods and droughts phenomena of wonder? How would our lives change if we adapted our culture to its constraints? Could we do this?

In the 1970s, in the early days of globalisation, climate change and the rush to get rich, two Australians gave serious consideration to these questions and the physical and social requirements for the restoration of Earth and sustainable living. This was permaculture – a contemporary response with universal application.

Chapter 6 notes

1 Pelletier, W. and Poole, T. *Wherever you are is home. Earth Prayers from Around the World.* Harper, SanFrancisco, 1991.

2 Skuthorpe, Tex and Sveiby, Karl-Erik. *Treading Lightly: The Hidden Wisdom of the World's Oldest People,* Allen & Unwin, Crows Nest, NSW, 2006, p. 18.

3 ibid.

4 At the Australian Permaculture Convergence, Kuranda, September 2010, an Aboriginal man, Seith Fourmile, Bimuy Walubara Yidinji, referred to the period of British occupation as the Age of Ecosystem destruction.

5 Amanda Cuyler and I recorded and filmed this and will have material ready for publication next year.

6 Fontana, Bernard. *Of Earth and Little Rain.* University of Arizona Press, Tucson. 1980.

7 Tobais, M. *Desert Survival by the Book.* New Scientist, 17 December, 1988.

8 Van Der Post, Laurens. *The Lost World of the Kalahari.* Penguin Books, Australia. 1958

7. Permaculture: to restore the Earth

Our heritage as human beings means we use human energy and spirit to design kind and generous landscapes.

In the early 1970s Bill Mollison and his student, David Holmgren, saw the global climate threat from environmental pollution and resource depletion. They studied ecology, the newest applied science and the first integrating science. They were like bowerbirds. They worked from the ecological imperative that *humans are part of nature, not above it and, ignore it at their peril.*

Delicately they put together a structure they called 'permaculture' referring to permanent culture and agriculture. They started with ethics then worked out principles for restoring and sustaining life in nature's systems and in human institutions. Declaring ethics up front was almost unknown at that time.

The permaculture ethics are to:
- care for the Earth
- care for people
- share/distribute everything surplus to our needs.

Quakers will recognise some permaculture principles as similar to their testimonies.
- practise right livelihood
- ethical use of money
- co-operation not competition
- build community strength and resilience.

Permaculture took the best from traditional cultures. They threw into the collation ways of thinking critically and creatively about water, soils, climate, weather, plants, forests; and human institutions affecting communities, cities, wealth, land tenure and ethics. They approached it from a clear understanding of the threats to Earth's health from global warming, land degradation, water pollution and forest depletion.

The thread that wove it all together was design consisting of three parts.

Firstly, an integrated and comprehensive analysis of a landscape and its society;

secondly, the design or pattern which addresses the problems found in analysis and restores Earth to health;

thirdly, the strategies and techniques required for implementing the design.

Their students were excited: they now had a restoration process. This was the first time in known human history that abundance and repair could be designed into productive human landscapes anywhere on Earth.

The two outstanding gifts of permaculture as the key to restoring land and human settlements are:
- design by principles
- integration of systems and elements essential to the design.

In a permaculture landscape, restitution of permanent forests and waterways is a priority.
- Encircle villages and towns by forested commons providing timber

and non-timber products, cleansing the water and filtering the air.
- Buildings are made of local materials and use renewable energies.
- Each town, farm and city has its own garden and possibly shared orchards. All organisms live within their rainwater budget and all water is recycled, cleaned and returned to its origins.
- Needs are met locally; imports are few.
- Maintenance work is replaced by productive work and time exists for arts and crafts.

This design, adapted to different climates and cultures, has become the basis for a worldwide movement of home, school and community gardens and eco-villages. I knew permaculture would be relevant to situations as diverse as:
- Vietnam's 30 million bomb craters
- toothpick-thin Cambodian landmine victims
- East Timorese passivity after colonial occupation, resistance and genocide
- Ethiopians confused by wars, communism and several regimes
- Ugandans' trauma from civil war and AIDS
- Albanians lost and destabilised by harsh Communism
- Malawi devastated from AIDS and war
- Homeless women and children in Kabul
- Vietnamese refugees in barbed wire and cement refugee camps.

With permaculture, my concern now had all its facets and it was finely applicable for people and cultures that endure or survive extreme conditions. Once equipped with permaculture, and understanding the priorities of need that lead to land restoration, I became a teacher, passionate about adult non-formal education and understanding that that was the sustainable way to pass on and localise knowledge. I was profoundly grateful for permaculture knowledge and skills and a rejoinder to the commandment to 'subdue the Earth', and it was to have benefits other than food and water security which I had not imagined.

8. Gardening the world back to health

The seed in the soil, the dirt on our hands
is the story I know and the song my soul understands.

Scientists are predicting worldwide food shortages.[1] Food shortages, once unknown in some countries where I work, are now common. And food shortages already exist where there is war, famine, land degradation, over-exploitation of resources and population pressure.

Inability to provide food for themselves is, for most of the world's people, a grave disempowerment (and should be for us Australians).

Gardening holds the possibility: from recovery of war-scarred landscapes to the restoration of the planet and global culture. James Strong[2] is a member of the NSW Meeting and said there is a theological message here, a rejoinder to the biblical command[3] to 'subdue the earth!' Something is needed to re-start the lives of people who survive trauma with lands destroyed and human spirit diminished; something which can meet physical, psychological, creative and spiritual needs.

Food is the bond that ties us to the soil and connects us with water and all other living things and it meets many human needs. In Abraham Maslow's[4] hierarchy of human needs, gardening would be at the bottom of the pyramid for the level of physical survival, and at the apex for the level of self-actualisation. Permaculture's strategies and skills are more about gardening than large scale agriculture. Permaculture is more about biodiversity and one thousand gardens than one garden for a thousand people.

Permaculture is about the gardener in an intimate relationship with soil, water, plants and animals.

Cambodia's story

During the Khmer Rouge regime in Cambodia the people suffered complete deprivation – land, family, food, freedom, health and education – and emerged often only with their lives. They had endured torture, brutality, beatings, starvation and being worked to extreme exhaustion.

People in every trade, profession and job had been killed. The survivors – depressed, mutilated, and dependent on each other to survive – were cut off from the world. They were anxious, uncertain about their future and the government, and appeared passive and unco-operative. They were apathetic and lived with unavoidable distress. They were thin, hungry, and had lost trust in themselves. They were traumatised by death and deprivation.

But they had survived and brought human resilience to peace. But they emerged into a different world and did not know where to start.[5]

Whatever the catastrophe, I recognised this pattern in each country where I worked.

Post-traumatic stress is recognised for 'our' people but sometimes not for others. In Vietnam, Cambodia and Albania, all the people were, and many are still, severely traumatised.

In Uganda and Cambodia in the first year of the project villagers wanted to plant annual vegetables but not fruit trees because they did not believe in a future.

People were starving in Cambodia, Ethiopia and Vietnam, and food was an enormous preoccupation. Women in Cambodia didn't want to attend gender or literacy classes. They spoke of lying awake at nights worrying what their children would eat. Their single focus was on food for which they had to forage for long hours.

They attended permaculture classes, returned home and immediately put it into practice. Permanent food gardens helped relieve them of fatigue and food uncertainty.

I will always remember the silence of Ethiopian women, at the end of their resources, sitting by the roadside surrounded by their small children. They knew nothing else to do once there was no more food in the grain store or the fields. They were quiet and passive.

By the time I arrived in Ethiopia I had had much experience and knew to start training immediately. A short time later I found that every Monday morning the newly trained Ethiopians were teaching batches of 18 village women how to begin and sustain a home garden. The gardens looked good.

We, through QSA had offered Cambodia and Vietnam a permaculture program over several years. Offering permaculture under these conditions we always start with food and water. All other gardening activities follow.

One and half years later Cambodian women had established nurseries, water systems, seedbanks, irrigation canals, and markets; but, first and foremost, food.

In countries with permaculture projects, hunger has always been relieved. Once there are local trainers the knowledge is left embedded in the community and new livelihoods created.[6] And after three months malnutrition declines.

Gardening in times of drought, pandemics or war rejects the chaos, and affirms human perseverance. Gardens are psychologically optimistic signs of regenerative spirit.

They restore the makers as much as they restore the landscape. Within a short time gardeners added flowers.

Immediately after the Khmer Rouge soldiers capitulated in 2002, we took gardening to Veal Veng district in Cambodia where the people were disoriented and starving. They began to garden immediately. Their gardens represented places and symbols of peace, anticipating peacetime and normalcy and allowing rest and privacy to reflect and process their experiences.

They offered peace, not merely as the absence of conflict but a positive, assertive state and welcome respite where *a moment's contemplation of nature helped restore one's peace of mind with greater efficacy than any man-made drug.*[7]

By taking possession of gardens dispossessed people re-capture satisfaction, self-respect and pride. They refute homelessness, helplessness and despair by identifying with a more settled future and their accomplishments. As gardens grow so do spirits.

In his autobiography, *Long Walk to Freedom*, Nelson Mandela[8] mentioned the garden he nurtured during his years in prison.

Creating a garden requires deliberate mental and physical activities attuned to soil, plant and seasonal rhythms and changes. Gardening is a 'head and hand' life and by putting food on the table people feel accomplished and empowered. Gardens are also about the simple and profound pleasure of fresh fruit and vegetables

Part of a garden's value is its ordinariness and necessity. The ordinary restores physical and psychological stability through awareness of life's regularities, and trust that the sun will rise, seasons change and the natural world continue.

Psychological healing results from several issues, among them:
- strong sense of accomplishment
- detachment from daily anxiety
- living in the moment
- integrating needs and place
- achieving a livelihood
- contributing to community
- engaging mind and body
- giving health, identity and purpose.

At community level and sites, gardening restores cultural integrity and self-respect.

Gardening has aesthetic and practical outcomes. Where before there were bombsites, gardens become places to gather, sit, play and work. They also ameliorate extremes of climate by creating microclimates with shade and comfort as relief from heat and dust.

This was really important in the orphanages of Uganda where there was dust and no shade. For people who have lived with ugliness and degradation, gardens are an outlet for creativity and artistry. Flowers for the pagoda were a priority in Cambodia and for the family altar in Vietnam where flowers for ancestor worship and simple beauty are highly regarded.

Where people have been depersonalised they can personalise their community and restore generosity. The poorest person can make an offering to the community.

How people adapt permaculture

From East Timor to Uganda new permaculturists naturally drew on their artistry and traditions to locally adapt and restore their environment and culture.

In Cambodia the program initiated community planning to transform towns and reclaim cultural continuity. Permaculture promoted non-political, impersonal co-operation and friendship where there was a recent heritage distrust and silence.

In Vietnam, permaculture merged perfectly with the doi moi[9] supported re-introduction of 3,000 years of cultural knowledge of horticulture and animals in diverse ecosystems. It was also a meaningful community activity for Vietnamese returning to flattened villages and landscapes. Gardening was a way everyone could contribute to building the new society. And they quickly grew huge quantities of food and reorganised markets. In Quang Binh farmers made gardens in pure sand with leaky fishponds.

The Khmer had been forced to make compost for the Khmer Rouge and hated it so we introduced composting that seemed a different activity and because they did not like the circle mandala gardens they made 'square' ones.

In Afghanistan where there was no compost or animal manure for nutrient, human effluent was used to grow the first plants to make the first compost.

And in Bavi province, Vietnam, the Dao were partners in a QSA project. They received fruit trees but on one monitoring visit they reported that some people had come from far away and stolen them. Later I sat in the kitchen with the women who told me they had given some trees to their neighbours, the Muong, who had none. They feared to tell us because they knew westerners didn't share like that.

In East Timor forest gardening assists adjustment to their fragile independence. It has medium range goals with real and simple expectations while providing solace for grief and loss, even imbuing psychological and political defiance.

Above all, permaculture restores food and water.

Within 12 weeks farmers and villagers can have about 50 per cent more food on their table. Malnutrition is visibly reduced. In Cambodia, in a very stretched village of mainly women and children, the people were plagued by tropical ulcers in the hunger season just before rice harvest. They learned to grow food with grey water and in a short time had flourishing small intensive gardens of about 15 species but there was no change in their health. The women trainers went to the village and simply told all participants to make and eat vegetable soup every lunchtime. Within six weeks, the ulcers were clearing up and their skin looked golden again.

Nature's resilience and mercy

Permaculture essentially mandates that every farm, village and town restore their native indigenous species. This re-wilding is critical to combat global warming and land degradation. Local species will adapt and survive under changing climate conditions. They protect from the elements and produce usable goods. In these natural areas pollinators and seed dispersers live. This is design by 're-wilding' the environment. Now strongly supported by governments and NGOs it allows nature to respond to environmental pressure. In Ethiopia when we discussed restoring wildlife corridors, the Konso were afraid of the return of lions to the villages until we renamed them biodiversity corridors. Then they were acceptable. The techniques for re-wilding are different from food gardening because nature can be trusted to renew herself if stress is removed.

A friend reminded me that gardeners work at the mercy of nature. Nature obscures evidence of human action. It may take generations but eventually culture becomes compost. It is a great solace that one day nature will cover the damage we do.

After widespread spraying and dumping of Agent Orange, I saw Vietnamese farms growing only bamboo and jackfruit. These were the only two species that would grow on toxic land and so the landscape became a poignant reminder of war. In the bomb craters peppering the landscape, Vietnamese farmers made fishponds.

In Afghanistan, grapes sprouted from war-stripped black trunks. A green flag is placed where each Afghani died, and where landmines exploded the land grows more beautiful as nature claims and dresses the land.

In Vietnam today most modern visitors are unaware of the bloodied ground beneath their feet and so are ignorant of nature's power to restore the tortured landscape to its former ecosystems.

Around shrines and cemeteries gardens are a constant affirmation of consecration. Every village war memorial in Vietnam has a small garden with food and flowers contributing to the idea of sacred and secular. By comparison Cambodia seems impoverished without local memorial gardens.

Restoring gardens, farms and towns after devastation hastens the process of removing signs of trauma. It is like applying a healing balm to the land.

As I consciously create gardens in the face of land degradation, war, peak oil and global warming I find that permaculture fulfils most needs of humans and other species from the most basic to the psychological and spiritual. This was reflected in the 2000 American Friends Service Committee (AFSC) Community Gardening Association in Bosnia and Herzegovina whose objectives were to:
- assist with material assistance for families by providing food and produce to sell
- offer work therapy and education, especially for children
- lessen the memory of former minefields and killing grounds

- establish priority for multi-ethnic people and orphans as members
- let the gardens herald the future and establish a different past
- let society move on.

There is profound satisfaction in working with permaculture but working under these confronting circumstances is not easy. After Afghanistan, despite outward success I went into a spiritual darkness.

Chapter 8 notes

1 Shiva, Vandana, *Food, Finance and Climate, Triple Crisis, A Three-fold Opportunity*, 2008, www.movementgeneration.org/food-finance-climate

2 James Strong is a member of Sydney Local Meeting and we had several rich conversations and helpful emails. They are personal communications.

3 Holy Bible, *Genesis* 1-28

4 http://en.wikipedia.org/wiki/Abraham Maslow's_hierarchy_of_needs

5 Oats, WN, *I Could Cry for These People: An Australian Quaker Response to the Plight of the People of Cambodia, 1979 - 1993*, Quaker Service Australia, North Hobart, Tasmania, 1994.

6 Evaluation of QSA permaculture projects

7 Helphand, Keith, *Defiant Gardens,* Trinity University Press, San Antonio, Texas, 2006, p. 174.

8 Mandela, Nelson, *Long Walk to Freedom*. Little Brown, Boston. 1994.

9 doi moi is defined as the 'post-war opening out to the world'.

9. Spiritual darkness

We have forgotten who we are.
We have alienated ourselves from the unfolding of the cosmos.
We have become estranged from the movements of the earth
We have turned our backs on the cycles of life.
We have forgotten who we are.
UN Environmental Sabbath Program[1]

A headline from the *New York Times*[2] newspaper-on-line read *Should this be the last generation?* The article by ethicist Peter Singer asked, *Is it in the best interests of children to be born into the deteriorating world we have made?*

I was shocked, despite having sometimes imagined the world without humans. But consciously to propose our cessation/extinction – the species which is reflective and thoughtful and creative?

The deteriorating world Peter Singer speaks of is one of accelerating loss and disruption of non-renewable resources and processes that took billions of years to evolve and stabilise. He places the responsibility on humans.

The deep ecologists existed naturally in simpler times, but those of our age were influenced by Arne Naess, the Norwegian, who stated and wrote forcefully, that humans are enmeshed in the cycles of all nature and that to deny or ignore that leads us into danger. One such deep ecologist is John Seed, who like Ness strongly believes that humans are an integral, but never greater, part of Nature; he suggests that we simply accept that we are an ill-adapted species – and not feel regret or guilt because, after all, we are just one species among 30 million. Other organisms in the past caused mass major extinctions (MMEs) and we are as they are. It is just life.

I accept both views. I grieve when thinking others may never have the opportunity to experience life, nor humans have the chance to reach their potential.

Humans are both at the core of the problem and the solution.

I found in Kenneth Boulding's[3] lines below, which could have been written for this lecture, an exceedingly urgent call for change.

How can we wait the many a weary year
Before rock of pride and cruel hate,
Into fruitful earth disintegrate.
Sonnet VII

I saw the permaculture projects had been materially successful. But with success I saw organisations and individuals corrupted. That was a heavy burden because I had made close friends and yet had been a medium for their corruption. There is little guidance for this special development problem. The roots of corruption seem to lie in prosperity and materialism that we, mostly unwittingly, model.

The human spirit is diminished by terrible wars and appalling catastrophes and very few individuals meet the challenge to live rich, spiritual lives under adversity. War is particularly destructive with long-term consequences for the environment and society. Behind many international wars are civil wars and the impact of the war between North and South Vietnam is still very painful. So is the Khmer civil war.

The impacts can be very personal and so, for example, in Cambodia it was sad to find a grandmother burdening her grandson and his twisted foot with the karma of having been a Khmer Rouge soldier in his last life.

Afghani suffering changed the national character. I was able to compare the country from 30 years earlier. In 1972 I found a coherent, resilient, hospitable people and a sustainable environment. In 2002 I returned and found the earth scorched and the people angry, aggressive, depressed and traumatised. Adults would compete with orphans for an asprin or to have a scratch treated. Afghanistan is my idea of hell.

I saw how disasters reduce a country's ability to withstand undesirable foreign influences. Law and justice break down, friends steal or betray, officials cut forests, men traffic in women and children, and corrupt the military and police. The greedy and ruthless enter the vacuum and hard sell cigarettes, alcohol, pharmaceuticals, fertilisers, and live body parts.

With loss of respect for law the country loses confidence in its culture and ability to control its future. Foreign world monetary organisations direct fiscal policy and reconstruction with little regard for sustainability and blame the country for its poverty or inability to cope with their decisions.

I have worked the hard way especially the last few years. I have been alone without those splendid comforting luxuries of the humanitarian work organisation: the car, the driver, the interpreter and the lovely person who organises your meals and needs. I have lacked a protective layer of skin over the raw nerves of life. And often lacked anyone to discuss seering experiences with.

I saw all of this and then with sadness fatigue I began to lose faith.

I went to Quakers and found no satisfactory theology of suffering and evil to explain the apparent blind human wilfulness that continued a path to chaos and destruction. James Backhouse believed in Satan and I found psychological reasons to do so, but no Quaker response. In searching among Friends I found little interest in the question: What can we say about adversity, evil and suffering? We don't deal well with 'that not of God'.

Now, conscious of the damage we cause, how must we humans manage ourselves? Can we manage ourselves? We are likely to fall into chaos and pain. Are we sufficiently prepared?

Early Quakers who lived in almost constant war understood and experienced evil and suffering – they saw 'the devil and Satan' as the cause of evil. Tragedy, understood as the Will of God, fitted into a divine scheme. Today this is not our belief.

Now I interpret evil as the inability of humans to deal responsibly with freedom so allowing 'that not of God' to emerge. Social limits and constraints are necessary to keep human behaviour restrained. I was more terrified when restraint was absent and the gap filled by militia, than I was by landslides or landmines.

James Backhouse's[4] spirits often plunged and he recorded dark times and lack of hope in changing human behaviours and beliefs.

Destitute of a sense of Divine presence by which I have often been comforted (p.106) and, *much, oppressed, my own state one of great emptiness* (p.388)

What sustained him was the certainty that his work was in right ordering. I slipped into heart pain when I understood from my experience that human behaviour was leading to a sixth MME and 'that not of God' caused extreme suffering.

This challenged my Quaker beliefs in 'that of God in everyone' but I became more profoundly opposed to all types of violence because of the long shadow it leaves over individuals and nations. I became more conscious of it in myself and worked to minimise its impacts. (When I was home once a week I would stand alone with a Peace sign beside the bus stop in Katoomba.)

And completely paradoxically I held fiercely to the words on a tattered poster hanging on my wall. They are John Woolman's[5]

There is a principle placed in
The human mind which is
Pure and proceeds from God.
It is deep and inward,

Confined to no religion
Where the heart stands
In perfect sincerity.

And I found none of the religions could offer an understanding and worldview that made sense of what I had known until I found cosmology which presented me with an extremely long world view, wonder at evolution confirming that life is the one real miracle, and a spirituality for all times and places.

Cosmology traces the scientific history of Earth from its origins through its evolving complexity including the human development. In cosmology I found solace and learned that destruction and chaos have been part of all evolution and usually contain the seeds of future stability and richness. I let go of my small time perspective and took an evolutionary one. Cosmology also shows that change can come from anywhere, not necessarily where human minds think it will. I decided that being part of the solution was my task.

Chapter 9 notes

1 Roberts, Elizabeth and Amidon. Elias. *Earth Prayers from Around the World*. Harper, San Francisco. 1991.

2 *New York Times*, Section, Opinionator, 9 May 2010.

3 Kenneth Boulding, an outstanding 20th century Quaker who contributed in ideas and action to worship and peace. He wrote Sonnets based on the first line of Nayler's poem.

4 Backhouse, Sarah, *Memoir of James Backhouse by his sister*, 2nd edn, William Sessions, York, 1877.

5 John Woolman, American Quaker, 1770-1777. He travelled under an anti-slavery concern.

10. Slowing the descent: living adventurously

Come to the edge, he said.
We are afraid, they said.
Come to the edge, he said.
They came to the edge.
He pushed them ... and they flew.
Guillaume Apollinaire

And now we are dancing on the peaks of oil, fresh water, soil, biodiversity, global warming, population, consumption and food. Any one of these can collapse and take the others with it, along with whole societies and ecosystems. Too much momentum and destruction have gathered now so we probably cannot stop a collapse but we can make it slower and less catastrophic.

We have several strategies, sufficient science and technology to move towards a low resource future but it is the human frailties that will challenge it most.

Earth needs
- people with skills, knowledge, Earth spirituality, influence and peacemaking skills
- transition to low consumption of energy, food, water and non-renewable resources
- restoration of landscapes to assist climate stability.

As these needs for Earth restoration are met, we will think and live differently. We will:

Model different ways of living

Earth's future depends most on transforming our behaviour and thinking. For our children and all species we need now to model new possibilities. From past, present, secular and spiritual societies we know how to continue to inhabit Earth. It isn't easy but this is really the only option. There are several interacting strategies that will be most powerfully followed by establishing good models of voluntary frugality.

Observe our behaviour

See what is happening in our minds, then adapt thoughts, practices, ethics and even deeply held beliefs. Species and ecosystems survive when they observe (notice) change and then adapt. Those who don't adapt become extinct.

Adapt-in-place and localise our lives

By thinking locally, acting locally and impacting globally; by staying local in our work, leisure, economics and relationships we stay grounded and we make a huge reduction in resource use and create cohesive communities. This will mean dropping the present culture of entitlement of individuals to whatever resources they wish to one of communal sharing.

The Transition Towns movement is a community initiative and a child of the bio-regional teachings of permaculture. It prepares cities and communities for a low carbon future. It builds networks and hubs of interest and function, linking all parts of a town, for example food, economy, education and transport. It requires us to know our place.

We must love it and grow intimate with all its parts and 'pay the rent' through restoration of habitat, soils and water.

At home I pay rent to my magpie and I am rarely without a maggie somewhere near me. I acknowledge her by ensuring she has drinking water, grass seed and occasionally a tiny speck of cheese. I plant trees she likes to live in. I belong to her so I must look after her.

Change behaviour

Live as if there is little food, no coal, oil or town water. In the Friends' World Committee for Consultation (FWCC) Booklet *Faith and Action*, contributors discussing *James* 2 wrote that faith preceded action.

Equally, I find that faith often follows action. Psychology has given us the powerful knowledge that changing behaviour changes the habitual thinking patterns of the mind. It is also my experience from teaching permaculture that when people practise new behaviours then fresh attitudes emerge.

Embrace a psychology of possibility

A permaculture principle states this as 'see solutions not problems'. Drawing on the landmark work of psychologists and medical researchers, Ellen Langer, in *Counterclockwise*, shows how to open to what is possible instead of clinging to notions about what is not. We can do this by:
- studying what might be, rather than a describing what is
- freeing ourselves from constricting mindsets
- recognising the difference between what we can control and what we cannot
- asking ourselves 'how can we do it?' rather than 'can we do it?'

Then I opened my Regional Meeting minutes[1] and found the following[2].

This [prophetic imagination] is the capacity to see what is yet possible under the power of God rather than yielding to cynicism and despair or to a status quo, which is death warmed over. It is the capacity to know deeply that seeing the possibility of reconciliation and of restoration is not merely lofty idealism or wishful thinking ... It is Jeremiah buying a field while he is in prison and the Babylonians are conquering his homeland, including the field. (Jeremiah 32)...

It is to hold out the real possibility that the future of our lives in the real world need not be bound by the patterns and failures of the past, but that it can be creatively ordered and empowered by the sovereign God who is with us in love.

Live community

Only collectively can we build resilience and restore Earth. We need networks of eco-communities, from neighbourhoods to intentional communities of life and spirit. Quakerism holds some of the necessary complexity and diversity that is communal strength, and a testimony to community. We cannot survive alone.

Evolutionary genetics explains[3] that there is a gene for altruism which needs altruistic people to work together because its strongest expression is through groups. Whereas one altruistic individual can be overcome by non-altruistic others, altruistic communities become strong forces for good. Quakerism holds a large bank of altruism.

Reinforcing this we know that humans are more responsive to change and adaptation when they engage in discussion and group action.[4]

In her essay, transition culture activist, Sharon Astyk, in *The Role of Religious Communities in the Long Emergency*[5] discusses how existing, self-reliant religious communities may serve both as blueprints and disaster response centres during times of crisis.

The whole project of Adapting-In-Place involves using what you've already got, and one of the tools [we] have is religious infrastructure which provides special things that few other institutions in our society do. The reality is that few secular institutions are prepared to fill the needs that people have in moments of crisis. This is what religious communities tend to do very well. They offer people access to familiar, structural ways to deal with events that change your world ...

> *Religious communities will have a large and powerful role in the future; one that ideally, we'd begin shaping and preparing for today. Because in many ways, they provide an existing infrastructure that is potentially powerfully adaptable to the life we will be living.*

I have reservations about her belief that religiously-based communities are automatically good for everyone. It depends on group culture and including values that accept diversity and difference.

Train ourselves

Learn negotiation and mediation skills to cope with potential conflicts over shortage of resources. It is probable that lack of these skills might finally determine how well we shift to a low energy and resource future.

At the heart and hands of change and adaptation are the Universe Story and The Great Work.

Chapter 10 endnotes

1 NSW Regional Meeting minutes, June 2010

2 Howard R. Macy, 1996 in Catherine Whitmire's *Practicing Peace*, 2007. p. 200, reprinted by Wahroonga LM, June 2010.

3 Radio National 'Late Night Live' Monday September 20, 2010

4 Robinson, Les and Glanznig, Andreas, *Enabling Ecoaction: A Handbook for Anyone Working with the Public on Conservation*, Humane Society International, WWF Australia, World Conservation Union, Sydney, 2003.

5 March 2009 blog entry on her website. http://sharonastyk.com/2009/03/19/the-role-of-religious-communities-in-the-long-emergency/

11. The unfolding universe story

Human completion, wholeness or religious awakening depends on a receptive opening up to the potentialities and sacred mysteries in the immediate natural environment.
Joseph Epes Brown

I have always found the Bible difficult, like reading someone else's story. I found it difficult to escape from the cultural and time-bound nature of religion. Pre-biblical religions must have contained truths as profound and universal as any we have. Every culture has its story of its origins and now we have been given another sacred story of universal significance.

All of us, every cell and leaf, virus, stone, wind and elephant share one Great Story and belong to it. All our origins are eternal with spiritual and physical potential for life to evolve with increasing complexity and diversity present at the birth of the universe. We share the same matter formed at the beginning of time. The question is not whether scientists can find the divine in religion but whether the religious can find the divine in science.

The work by Catholic Earth theologians Brian Swimme[1] and Thomas

Berry drew on Matthew Fox and earlier theologians such as Hildegard von Bingen and St Francis d'Assisi.[2] As theologians, astronomers and paleontologists they traced the unfolding of our universe, the birth and growth of Earth and her evolution and all species living on her. It does not negate existing religions but extends them further. In fact Swimme discusses cosmology from a Christian viewpoint.

This unfolding universe story enthralled me. Of startling relevance to Earth's future are the synchronicities and the wonders: the beauty, the co-operation and cataclysms and I loved the forward movement of it, the miraculous and transcendent that made it the spiritual story I had been searching for.

This cosmological story requires that we forge relationships with life and is, for me, more miraculous and awe-inspiring than Bible stories. We need relationships of trust, love, sharing and respect with every element of life.

Adapting and restoring life creates a role for us. Nature requires of us tenderness, appreciation and love of our eco-communities – relationships that discourage a *take* mentality or a culture of entitlement.

Singh, writing about Hendryk Skolimowski[3], gives a cosmic Indian understanding of how we must live. Skolimowski does not think of time-bound programs. He thinks in millennia and not merely of the human race but the welfare of all species on Earth.

The chapter, Cosmocracy, from Singh's book, *Philosophy for a New Civilisation*, explains how

> *Universal democracy, when it is extended to all beings, becomes Cosmocracy. Cosmocracy simply signifies the recognition that all powers come from the Cosmos. Celebrating the Cosmos as the power-giver leads to a political system which acknowledges those tremendous forces which brought life and human societies to existence. Our global ecumenical thinking must inform us that we are all connected within the stupendous tapestry of the evolving Cosmos. This recognition must inform us that seeking justice, freedom and the good life cannot be confined to a few select societies.*

Taking cosmology further is the essentially mystical Universe Story[4] in which science opens to divine inspiration – especially valuable for those religions which encourage revelation. Quakers would find the story a natural extension of their beliefs and testimonies. For religions which believe that all revelation is contained in their sacred book and there is none outside it, this may not be acceptable. Quakers hold with continuing revelation.

The unfolding Universe Story leads naturally to the Great Work – our great work to join the web of life as equal members and to engage in a new and restorative, reflective role.

Chapter 11 notes

1 *Earth Light* was an Earth Theology journal produced by Friends in Unity with Nature (FUN) for about 10 years, now discontinued. I have most copies.

2 Twelve episodes of *Canticle to the Cosmos*, DVD series, USA Institute of Ecology and Spirituality

3 Singh's Paper on Hendryk Skolimowski

4 Berry, Thomas, *Dream of the Earth*, Sierra Club Books, San Francisco, 1996.

12. The great work of restoration and reflection

To treat life as no less than a miracle is to give up on it.
Wendell Berry

The great unfolding Universe Story leads us to explore the role of humans on Earth; a new role, not as stewards, guardians or ministers at which we have manifestly failed. Entering into this relationship of reciprocity with Earth our work will be humble, respectful and restorative.

Earth gives everything good such as clean air, water, soil, food and timber but we must restore and replenish them in good order. Restoration means more than sustaining. We must replace 20 per cent more to all environments than we take, whether it is water supply and storage, or forests or wildlife habitat. This is will give some intergenerational equity.

And our other role is to reflect.

What we have to offer is wonder, consciousness and gratitude. We are the conscience of Earth. She has no other. It must be a sensitive conscience based on pattern literacy.

To do this we must learn the patterns and relationships in nature, integrating ourselves into them and becoming Earth literate. We largely ignore ever-changing colours, shapes, homes, food, temperature, air quality and insects.

It is thrilling beyond imagination that a deeper layer exists in the interactions occurring among all parts.

The inter-relationships and interdependencies in one backyard on an ordinary day are amazing and confounding; dramas, conflicts and resolutions are played out in the minute and the gigantic.

All life is patterns within patterns for every function of life; patterns of growth and death; patterns which, as they become visible, we will see as miracles. That all lives are lived in patterns with mathematical relationships is miraculous. Nothing is outside a pattern.

These underlying patterns supporting life from conception to growth are always different yet always the same. The essential pattern is the network sharing pattern which links all.

The nature of Nature is sharing the glue holding together all patterns and relationships.

We all know the generosity and liberality of Nature.

Everyday we see her abundance and co-operation working in pollen transfer, nectar, whale song, songs, dances, rescues, harvest, planting and distributing, joy and surplus.

Both teaching and learning are essential experiences of sharing. Speech, labour, ideas, food, thinking: all are shared through talk or body language.

Life could not have evolved without co-operation being a much greater force than competition. Our tendencies toward goodness are innate.

The paradox of sharing is that if we share with our neighbours who have less we gain more than if we had kept it all for ourselves. Sharing is a basic pattern-forming process ... shapes harmonious relationshisp in animal and human life. There is a 'manna' of sharing throughout nature. Boundaries are blurred. [1]

Traditional societies demonstrate sharing as a virtue for survival, apart from its moral and spiritual richness. Sharing is elevated to a significant community survival value. Social resilience, necessary for survival, needs effective networks. Enabling, and never inhibiting these relationships among all life is our job.

With the Great Work our relationship with Earth and reflective consciousness will change human interactions – a creative and exciting challenge.

The Australian Earthcare Statement starts with this relationship. Some of us know what is required to be in this relationship and hesitantly develop intimacy in our niche because this is where we need to start.

It has taken us a long time to get to an environmental testimony and we struggle to live it. We believe in letting our lives speak but it is no longer a question of living simply, but living frugally. We need to cut our consumption of almost everything by 90 per cent for Earth to have a chance of surviving.

This calls for radical witness. Are we willing to do it?

We have scarce time and will and cannot call upon God to fix this situation. The future will have scarcity and hardship. Not to change now will only jeopardise Earth's future well-being.

As Quakers, our history and testimonies strongly support moving to a new witness and relationships. Earth desperately lacks communities of witness to restoration and new ways of living on Earth.

My message is:

Earth is restorable and retrievable. With the new story the Great Work is the most important thing we can undertake.

Will children of the future generations thank us for passing on Earth with all her systems and species intact and healthy? I don't know, but we know how to do it and the time is short.

I must sign off and walk with the challenges:
Will we love this Earth?
Will we restore her?
And will we live with her in peace and prosperity?

You shall go out with Joy
And be led forth in peace,
And the mountains and hills
Will burst into song before you
And trees of the field
Will clap their hands.
Isaiah 55:12

Chapter 12 endnotes
1 Turnbull, Colin, psychologist *The Forest People* File Format: PDF/Adobe Acrobat Simon & Schuster, 1987.

References

Aboriginal Law Bulletin, May 1966, Vol. 3, Special Women's Issue.

Angyal, Andrew, J. Thomas Berry's Earth Spirituality and the Great Work from Scientific and Religious Perspectives on Altruism. Published in *The Ecozoic Reader*, s 3(2003) 35-44. http://www.ratical.org/man_worlds/GreatWork html

AYM Faith & Practice Committee, *Quakers and Nature* 'Friends' Writings which have drawn inspiration from creation and the environment', O'Connor, ACT, 1996.

AYM, *This We Can Say: Australian Quaker Life, Faith and Thought*, AYM Religious Society of Friends (Quakers) Inc., Armadale, Victoria, 2003.

Backhouse, James, *A Narrative of a Visit to the Australian Colonies*, published in London, 1843.

Backhouse, Sarah, *Memoir of James Backhouse by his sister*, 2nd edn, William Sessions, York, 1877.

Bane, Peter, ed. Education, *Permaculture Activist,* Issue No. 53, Autumn 2004.

Bayes, Helen, *Prophetic Community*, Canadian Quaker Pamphlet No. 69, Argenta Friends Press, 2009.

Bayliss-Smith & Feachem, R. 'Subsistence and Survival, Rural Ecology in the Pacific.' *The Structure of Permanence: The Relevance of Self-subsistence Communities for World Ecosystem Management*, William C. Clare. Chapter 12, Academic Press, 1977.

Berry, Thomas, *Reinventing The Human*, Talk delivered in Chapel Hill NC, June 1997.
> *The Ecozoic Era*, 11th Annual Schumacher Lectures, October 1991.
> www.schumachersociety.org/publication.html
> *The Dream of the Earth*, Sierra Club Books, San Francisco, 1988.
> www.sierraclub.org/books
> The Universe as Sacred, *Earthsong Journal*, Autumn, 2005.

Boulding, Kenneth, *There is a Spirit: The Nayler Sonnets*, Fellowship Publications, NY, 1979.

Brindle, Susannah, To Sing a New Song, *James Backhouse Lecture,* Religious Society of Friends (Quakers) 2000.

Brown, Peter & Garver, Geoffrey, *Right Relationship: Building a Whole Earth Economy*, Berrett-Koehler Publishers, Inc. San Francisco, USA, 2009.

Brown, Shirley, Report from local BLUFM radio. Private email June 2010.

Cable, Mildred with French, Francesca, *The Gobi Desert*, Hodder and Stoughton, London, 1943.

Catholic Earthcare, *On Holy Ground: An Ecological Vision for Catholic Education in New South Wales Australia* www.catholicearthcareoz.net - ecological principles: right to a safe ecological environment is a universal human right.

Carson, Rachel, *A Sense of Wonder*. Film by Haskell Wexler on Carson's life. *Silent Spring*, Penguin, 1962.

Church of England, *Book of Common Prayer*.

Climate Change: http://www.colombia.edu/-jeh1/ Dr James Hansen, Australian Bureau of Meteorology and CSIRO – Joint Statement http://www.csiro.au/resources/State-of-the-Climate.html

Connor, Lizzie, *Our Seven Ages* 'An unfolding story of human evolution since the beginning of our Universe', Katoomba, 2007. oursevenages.blogspot.com/

Davis, Wade, Sacred Geography *The Wayfinders – Why Ancient Wisdom Matters in the Modern World*, 4th Massey Lecture, Radio National, 2010.

De Blas, Alexandra, Making the Shift: from consumerism to sustainability: *ECOS* (CSIRO magazine), No. 153, Feb/Mar 2010 www.ecosmagazine.com

Deasey, Mark, *To do Justly and to Love Mercy: Learning from Quaker Service*, James Backhouse Lecture, Religious Society of Friends (Quakers) 2002.

Devall, Bill & Sessions, George, *Philosophy of Technology* 2010. http://www.transnational-perspectives.org/transnational/articles/article36.pdf

Dillard, Annie, *Pilgrim at Tinker Creek*, Penguin, 1982.

Drengson, Alan, 'Ecophilosophy, Ecosophy and the Deep Ecology Movement: An Overview', 1999. An earlier version of this article appeared in *The Trumpeter: Journal of Ecosophy*, Vol. 14, No. 3, Summer 1997, pp 110-111, entitled 'An Ecophilosophy Approach, the Deep Ecology Movement, and Diverse Ecosophies'. http://trumpeter.athabascau.ca

Edwards, Charles, *Resilient Nation*, Demos, document on line.

Ellegird, Alvar, *Science in the nineteenth century*, University of Cambridge Press, 2004. http:www.cambridge.org

Fontana, Bernard, *Of Earth and Little Rain*, University of Arizona Press, Tucson, 1989.

Freire, Paulo, *Pedagogy of the Oppressed*, Penguin Books, Australia, 1972.

FWCC, *Faith and Action Study Booklet*, Autumn 2010. www.fwccawps.org

Fox, George, *George Fox Journal*, Rufus Jones edition, 1908, p. 97.

Fox, Paul, *Clearings: Six Colonial Gardeners and the Landscapes*, The Miegunyah Press, Carlton, Victoria, 1994. www.mup.com.au

Gates, Bill, Innovations to Zero, TED, March 2010.

Gould, Helen, *The Quaking Meeting*, James Backhouse Lecture, Religious Society of Friends (Quakers), 2009.

Green, Barbara & Gollancz, Victor, *God of a Hundred Names*, Gollancz Paperbacks, 1985.

Hamilton, Clive, *The Freedom Paradox: Towards Post-Secular Ethics*, Allen and Unwin, Crows Nest, NSW 2008. www.allenandunwin.com.

Hellum, A.K. *Listening to Trees*, NeWest Press, Edmonton, Alberta, Canada, 2008.

Hill, Stuart, 'Redesigning agroecosystems for environmental sustainability: a deep systems approach'. Correspondence to Stuart B. Hill, Faculty of Social Inquiry, Social Ecology Group, University of Western Sydney, Hawkesbury, Locked Bag #1, Richmond, NSW 2753, Australia.

Holt-Gineny, Eric & Patel, Raj, *Food Rebellions: Crisis and Hunger for Justice,* 2008, on-line.

Intrator, Sam M. (Ed) *Living The Questions: Essays inspired by the work and life of Parker J. Palmer,* Jossey-Bass, A Wiley Imprint, San Francisco, 2005. www.josseybass.com

Johnson, David, *Peace is a Struggle*: James Backhouse Lecture, 2005.

Leopold, Aldo, *A Sand Country Almanac,* Ballantyne Books, NY, 1949.

Levi, Primo, *If This is a Man,* Abacus, Sphere Books Ltd, 1987.

Mackie, Frederick, *Traveller Under Concern*: *The Quaker Journals of Frederick Mackie on his tour of the Australasian Colonies,* 1852-1855, University of Tasmania, 1973.

McHarg, Ian, *Design with Nature,* American Museum of Natural History, NY, 1967. Library of Congress Card No. 76-77344

Meitzner, Yoder, 'Resource Rights', *ECHO Development Notes,* January 2010. www.echonet.org

Merton, Thomas, *The Sign of Jonas,* Hollis and Carter, London, 1953.

Miller, Alex, 'More Than Just Mates – The Gift Economy and Friendship', *Australian Literary Review,* Issue 6, July 2009.

Mitchell, Elizabeth, Excerpt from Red Mitchell's diary. Unpublished private email June 2010.

Mollison, Bill, *Permaculture: A Designer's Manual,* Tagari Publications, Tyalgum, NSW, 1988.

Murdoch, Iris, *The Sovereignty of Good*, Penguin, London.

Nash, Roderick, *The Rights of Nature*: 'A History of Environmental Ethics', Primavera Press, The Wilderness Society, Leichhardt, Australia, 1990.

Naydler, Jeremy, 'The Work of a Gardener', *Resurgence Magazine*, No. 32, 1989.

New Internationalist, 'Mothers Who Die'. Issue 420, March 2009.

Orr, David, 'What is Education For?' Article in *The Learning Revolution*, No. 27, Winter 1991, p. 52, reprinted 1996, Context Institute. (David Orr is an environmental educator.)

O'Shea, Janey, *Living The Way: Quaker Spirituality and Community*, 28th James Backhouse Lecture, Religious Society of Friends (Quakers),1993.

Palmer, Parker, *Let Your Life Speak*, Jossey-Bass Inc, San Francisco, USA, 2000.
To Know as we are Known: 'Education as a Spiritual Journey', Harper, San Francisco.

Pelletier, W and Poole T, *Wherever You Are Is Home: Earth Prayers from Around the World*, Harper, San Francisco, 1991.

Pogue Harrison, Robert, *Gardens: An Essay on the Human Condition*, University of Chicago Press, 2008.

Rice, Edward, *The Man in the Sycamore Tree*: *The Good Times and Hard Life of Thomas Merton*, Image Books, Division of Doubleday, NY, 1972.

Roberts, Elizabeth & Amidon, Elias, *Earth Prayers from Around the World*, *Harper*, San Francisco, 1991. www.harpercollins.com

Rothwell, Nicolas, 'Into The Red', *The Monthly*, May 2009, pp.38-46.

Schor, Juliet, B & Taylor, Betsy, Ed. *Sustainable Planet*, 'Solutions for the twenty-first century', Beacon Press, Boston, 2002. ISBN0-8070-0455-3 www.beacon.org

Seligman, Martin, *Authentic Happiness*, 2002, p.119.

Shuford, John A. 'AVP – An Instrument of Peace', *American Friend*.

Singh, Vir, 'Fertilising the Universe – Sustainability as a Cosmic Quest?, Paper presented at Symposium on The New Horizons of Sustainability, India International Center, New Delhi, India, 12 March 2009.

Singer, Peter, *Ethics and Climate Change*, ABC Radio National, 5 pm, March 6, 2010.

Society of Jesus, *Seven Year Plan for Generational Change for the Society of Jesus*. Personal communication with Fr Paul Demarais, Zambia.

Stevenson, Charles, Ed. *As The Seed Grows: Essays in Quaker Thought*. Australia Yearly Meeting, Tasmania, 2007.

Swimme, Brian, *Canticle to the Cosmos*, Video Series, Institute for Spirituality and Ecology, California, 2006.

Sydney Morning Herald, 'We no longer turn to myths to assuage suffering', Nine Letters to the Editor on Evolution v. Creation, September 27, 2009.

Sveiby, Karl-Erik & Skuthorpe, Tex, *Treading Lightly: The Hidden Wisdom of the World's Oldest People*, Allen & Unwin, Australia, 2006.

Taylor, Jill Bolte, *My Stroke of Insight*, Hodder & Stoughton, UK, 2008.

Thurman, Howard, *Mysticism and the Experience of Love*, Pendle Hill Pamphlet No. 115, Woodford Library.

Van der Post, Laurens, *The Lost World of the Kalahari*, Penguin, London, 1968.

Walker, James, Backhouse, *Walk to the West*, Royal Society of Tasmania, 1992.

Watson, Elizabeth, *Guests of my Life*, Celo Press, Arthur Morgan School, Burnsville NC, 28714, 1979.

Westra, Bosselman, *Reconciling Human Existence and Ecological Integrity*, Earthscan.

Weil, Simone, *Two Moral Essays*, Pendle Hill Publication No. 240, 1981.

Whitman, Walt, *The Portable Walt Whitman*, Penguin Books, 1973.

Winton, Tim, *Land's Edge*, McMillan, Australia, 1993, p.44.

Woolman, John, 'Conversations on the True Harmony of Mankind and How it May be Promoted'.

Zethoven, Imogen, Origins and Evolution of the Sustainability Debate, Sustainable Development - A Critique of Perspectives. In Smith J.W. (1991, Ed.) *Immigration, Population and Sustainable Environment*, Flinders (SA), Australia. Imogen Zethoven, Great Barrier Reef Campaign Manager WWF: (07) 3839 2677; mobile 0414 950 959

Web links
01 to 10 http://www.quakers.org.au/displaycommon.cfm?an=1&subarticlenbr=264

01 Quaker Earthcare Statement, Australia Yearly Meeting 2008

02 Quaker Earthcare Action in Australia

02-1 Earthcare Action Network

02-2 Discussion Paper – Background to the proposal

03 Earthcare for Friends at Home

04 Quaker Earthcare for Meeting Houses

05 Quaker Earthcare for AYM gatherings

06 Quaker Earthcare for isolated Friends

07 Earthcare and the Quaker testimonies

08 Quaker Earthcare and AYM Peace & Legislation Committee

09 Quaker Earthcare with Indigenous concerns

10 Quaker Earthcare and Education

11 Quaker Earthcare & Junior Young Friends and Children of the Meeting. www.spont.com/earthcare.htm

12 Quaker Earthcare Action & Reflection By Young Friends. fwccawps.org/pubs/resources/2010_Australia%20YM.pdf

13 Friends' Earthcare action and events worldwide. qewnet.ning.com/forum/topics/un-info-unfccc-united-nations-1 -

14 Earthcare & Quaker Quotes.quakerearthcare.org/PDFs/Seeds_Vol_III.pdf

15 Understanding the reality of climate change. www.ukcip.org.uk/index.php?id=73&option=com

16 Ways of measuring ecological footprint.
www.wwf.org.au/footprint/

17. Films and documentaries.
www.earthcarefilms.com/docu/mn-docu.htm
www.earthcarefilms.com/docu/ls-cons.htm
www.earthcarefilms.com/docu/ls-devp.htm

THE **JAMES BACKHOUSE** LECTURES

1990	*Quakers in Politics: Pragmatism or Principle?* Jo Vallentine & Peter Jones
1991	*Loving the Distances Between: Racism, Culture and Spirituality*, David James & Jillian Wychel
1993	*Living the Way: Quaker Spirituality and Community*, UJ O'Shea
1994	*As the Mirror Burns: Making a Film about Vietnam*, Di Bretherton
1995	*Emerging Currents in the Asia-Pacific*, DK Anderson & BB Bird
1996	*Our Children, Our Partners – a New Vision for Social Action in the 21st Century*, Elise Boulding
1997	*Learning of One Another: The Quaker Encounter with Other Cultures and Religions*, Richard G Meredith
1998	*Embraced by Other Selves: Enriching Personal Nature through Group Interaction*, Charles Stevenson
1999	*Myths and Stories, Truths and Lies*, Norman Talbot
2000	*To Learn a New Song: A Contribution to Real Reconciliation with the Earth and its Peoples*, Susannah Kay Brindle
2001	*Reconciling Opposites: Reflections on Peacemaking in South Africa*, Hendrik W van der Merwe
2002	*To Do Justly, and to Love Mercy: Learning from Quaker Service*, Mark Deasey
2003	*Respecting the Rights of Children and Young People: A New Perspective on Quaker Faith and Practice*, Helen Bayes
2004	*Growing Fruitful Friendship: A Garden Walk*, Ute Caspers
2005	*Peace is a Struggle*, David Johnson
2006	*One Heart and a Wrong Spirit: The Religious Society of Friends and Colonial Racism*, Polly O Walker
2007	*Support for Our True Selves: Nurturing the Space Where Leadings Flow*, Jenny Spinks
2008	*Faith, Hope and Doubt in Times of Uncertainty: Combining the Realms of Scientific and Spiritual Inquiry*, George Ellis
2009	*The Quaking Meeting: Transforming Our Selves, Our Meetings and the More-than-human World*, Helen Gould
2010	*Finding our voice: Our truth, community and journey as Australian Young Friends*, Australian Young Friends

Backhouse Lectures, as well as other Australia Yearly Meeting publications, are available from Friends Book Sales, PO Box 181, Glen Osmond, South Australia, 5064, Australia. Email <sales@quakers.org.au>.

www.ingramcontent.com/pod-product-compliance
Ingram Content Group UK Ltd.
Pitfield, Milton Keynes, MK11 3LW, UK
UKHW042004230426
12048UKWH00009B/535